Painting Trees

Poems by Linda Jackson Collins

Published by:
   Random Lane Press
   Sacramento, CA
   randomlanepress@gmail.com

ISBN: 0-978-9978923-7-6

Cover Art: Angela Tannehill

Book Design: Angela Tannehill

Other poetry books from Random Lane Press:

Poet Warrior	by NSAA
Geographic Tongue	by Sarah Lagomarsino
The Way Back	by Mike Owens
Lift	by Connie Gutowsky
Standing Watch	by Stan Zumbiel
I line my life in dreams	by Ann Hsiao Keen
Inheritance	by Sarah Lagomarsino
Play	by Connie Gutowsky

Acknowledgments

I am grateful to Joyce Hsiao and Bob Stanley of
Random Lane Press for their generosity and support in
bringing this book and others into being.

Also, many thanks to these poets and writers who have
provided encouragement, inspiration, and gentle critiques:

Julie Bruck, Dave Boles, Leigh Anne Burford, Ed Cole, Julia Connor,
Cheryl Fuller, Bill Gainer, Jan Haag, Joyce Hsiao, Tim Kahl,
Susan Kelly-DeWitt, Kim Kralowec, Phillip Larrea, Laura Martin,
Josh McKinney, Geoffrey Neill, Bob Stanley

PCG Workshop members: Clare Bonsall, James Cooper,
Susan Flynn, Marcene Gandolfo, Carol Lynn Grellas, Connie Gutowsky,
Marie Reynolds, Ellen Yamshon, Stan Zumbiel

Rivertown Writers members: John Bell, Susan Davis,
Matt Johnson, Karin Erickson McClurg, Dorothy Rice,
Rick Robinson, KC Robinson, Ursula Stuter

Finally, love to my husband, Rob Collins, who encourages
all my hare-brained schemes even when they're not "his thing."

Contents

Some Sort of Reckoning 1

    Rainy Spell. 2

    Early Memory, Tributary 3

    Foxtails & Crystals 4

    How to Fly a Kite 6

    Flower Children 1969 7

    Live from the Surface of the Moon. 8

    Vietnam Memorial, Washington, D.C.. 9

    Spring Fancy. 10

Letting Go 11

    Letter to Louisville 12

    Vegetables. 14

    Theory of Absolutes 16

    Parallel Parking. 17

    Spackle 18

    Petrichor 19

    My Friend, Pluto 20

    Shoo Fly. 22

    Opihi 23

How It Comes to This 25

    Peace Line Wall 26

    Enlisted Men 27

    Last Suppers. 28

    In Service. 29

    Capital Airshow, September 11, ... 30

    The End Starts Before You Know It 32

    Seeing Nancy Pelosi at Café de la Presse. 34

Painting Trees 37

    Painting Trees. 38

    Reading Kwasny at 30,000 Feet 39

    On the Train to La Spezia 40

    Backstage with Balkanski Circus Dancers 41

    W.S. Merwin and Monet 42

    Amethyst Brook 44

    By the River Before Dawn. 45

    Letter to Kuusisto from California. .46

    path of totality 47

Overcomplicating Things 49

    Self-Portrait with Lemons. 50

    Daylight Savings. 52

    Marriage 53

    Moonlit. 54

    Homage to My Hair 55

    Crossed Signals 56

    Outside the Box 58

    Toolbox Letters. 59

Everything Keeps Shifting 61

    Distant 62

    Transition, Spring. 63

    Apples and Tomatoes. 64

    He Grows Old 65

    Early Blizzard 66

    Forward Light 67

    It's not as if you have to drink the sea 68

    Words Escape Her. 70

    A Second Life 71

Notes 72

Some Sort of Reckoning

Rainy Spell

Then I was rarely settled enough
to apprehend rain   often invisible
against a sheet metal sky
soundless beyond thick window
panes   until a taste of wetness in the air
a lingering mist   drops suspended there
among the fuchsia bells
showed me what I'd missed

These days   outside and still
first the blistering pond
then patter on leaves
like the ticking of timeless clocks

Shuddering sword-like stalks
seem to have slashed the sky
loosening this torrent of droplets
filling a hollowed bole

Petals resist the pelting

Blossoms like goblets catch
and spill   catch and spill
water disappears
into the earth together
with secrets buried there

Early Memory, Tributary

The creek behind our house
a bed of moss-sheathed stones.

Tangled roots, unruly grasses
bank the creek behind our house.

Behind our house in summer heat,
the creek, a slender snaking slick.

Crouched by the creek behind
our house, children fashion

dams from twigs, cup frogs in palms,
float popsicle stick boats.

Come winter, the swollen creek behind
our house mirrors sodden clouds.

Behind our house, where Jimmy toddles,
muddy water swirls, swallows.

Foxtails & Crystals

Winter
We meet at the top,
take turns on your Flexible Flyer.
My mom waves her warnings
as we barrel downhill,
beanie fringe blowing
like storm-battered birds.
This is some kind of daring.

Past the woodpile we plod
to a marshmallow drift. Inside
our snow-cave fort — pine cone décor,
mitten-smoothed walls —
we suck icicle spikes.
Crystals prickle our lips.
We speak in serious clouds.
Our words dissolve by dusk.

Summer

We meet in your back yard,
skin already sticky, t-shirts damp.
We slide down the bank to the water's edge,
then hop rocks to the other side
where we've built a ramshackle fort:
plywood walls, cracked plastic roof.
Foxtails tickle our legs
while we sip ritual water
from a shared tin cup.

We take turns on my purple Sears Spyder.
Your mom shouts in Russian,
scattershot scolding I can't understand.
Handlebar fringe flying,
we hurtle downhill
toward some kind of reckoning.

How to Fly a Kite

Have your best friend hold it overhead.
Then, unfurl a length of string —
enough to reach tree top height.
Do a count-down together.
When you reach blast-off,
run as fast as you can
trailing the string over your shoulder.
Your friend must toss the kite upward
at the exact moment
the string slack runs out.
Your job is to keep running
and paying out the line.
Your friend's job is to yell
and wave her arms in giant circles
to show the kite
that it is meant to climb —
that despite its tether
and its flapping ribbon tail
and power lines
and whistling wind
the kite's job is to ride the currents
higher and higher
as far as it can go
away from the smallness
of everything below.

Flower Children 1969

We weren't real hippies
still, we looked the part

feet hidden by bell bottom jeans
peace sign pendants bumping our chests

knees dusted by fringe
dangling from braided leather belts.

We sang *Marrakesh Express*
into microphone thumbs

shouted *make love not war*
at dads driving Buicks

shuffled through fiery yellow
and blood red leaves

giddy over the moon's "magnificent desolation"
and Nixon's troop withdrawals

in those autumn afternoons before we learned
of Charlie Company's savage rampage

and that *give peace a chance*
was only a song.

Live from the Surface of the Moon

Through our porthole into space
we see the LM's spider leg,
its ladder rungs blurred
against a stark, starless sky.
Nothing stirs, nothing sounds.
Angled shadows slice the silver curve.

We watch from Christine's den
this summer morning, thick as wool.
Her mother's worry fills the airless room,
but we girls track the screen unfazed.
We've known miracles before.

We want to see beyond
the TV's narrow frame, to know
if lunar sand makes castles too,
how it is to look at earth
from earth.

Soon the ghostly form descends,
white spongy suit, boxy PLSS.
He pauses on the lower rung —
dangles one boot above
that last vacant breadth.

    LM = Lunar Module, pronounced lem
    PLSS = Personal Life Support System, pronounced pliss

Vietnam Memorial, Washington, D.C.

There, camouflaged
      by green grass and dogwoods
cut into the landscape
           like the sides of a foxhole
great slabs of gabbro stone
        lengths tapered
        like the smoked steel of gun barrels
aim outward from an apex of grief.

To see that wall . . .
      motionless.
Arms outstretched
          like Christ on the cross.
Mirrored people kneeling,
        fingers brushing etched names,
their offerings,
      letters, dog-tags,
collecting at its feet.

Spring Fancy

These mornings come, arriving
in soft fibrous tendrils, branches, petals —

fertile seeds sprout, unfurl
seeking sunlight, pushing

through earth, away from what before
was everywhere but here

was gestating under these boundless fields
the loamy soil cloaked

in winter warmth, insulating snow
under the solitude of early moon.

As March frost thaws to April dew
and slender shoots emerge from muddy beds

we forget the thorns, the thistles,
the lingering of summer's hardened light.

Letting Go

Letter to Louisville

Summer nights relieved of heat.
Weeps of willows. Fireflies.
A trace of honey-almond phlox.
I am back there playing flashlight tag,
crouched in darkness
beneath chokeberry branches,
hugging my own thumping chest.
I want the boy wielding the flashlight
not to find me. Or maybe
I want him to find me.
What I do know is
his sly smile nettles
like the branches prickling my neck.

Another summer, another boy.
I have maneuvered to the seat next to his
at the Vogue's midnight show.
We sneak sips of smuggled bourbon,
make wisecracks under the screen's
flickering gloom. I wish
for his hand to reach for mine
but when he drapes his arm
across my shoulder,
I startle like a fawn.

August. Our canoes slice
the Ohio River's current.
Three boys, three girls, we paddle

to Six Mile Island's far side
where a knotted rope dangles
from a high alder branch.
We take turns. Pull the rope-end
up the embankment, grasp
its coarse braided strands.
Swing out over the murky inlet pool —
gliding, careless, the only hard part,
knowing just when to let go.

Vegetables

As a I child I didn't much like them
but in fairness, my mom served
the kind from cans. They'd slop
from her warming pan, slippery
army-green mush, unrecognizable
except those asparagus spears,
limp as worms. They'd form
a tepid pool of disappointment
I couldn't bring myself to swallow.

Forbidden to leave my laden plate,
I'd sit there suffering just as mightily
as those starving children in China —
until I learned that with a flick
of a fork, I could lob uneaten globs
into the space behind our fridge.
There they'd disappear like magic.

Clever me, I remember thinking
as Mom clucked approval
at my newly tractable ways —
until weeks later when our fridge broke down
and she called a repairman
who came the very next day (it was the 1960s),
a man of understatement who tugged
the fridge from the wall and said
here's your problem ma'am.

The evidence was undeniable:
stringy strands of spinach wrapped
around the coils and dried clumps
of sickly squash laid-out like a rebuke.
Mom's eyes narrowed at this triple
betrayal: not just my dirty trick,
but that I showed no signs of scurvy,
and that I wasn't sure those children
were starving after all.

Theory of Absolutes

inspired by Jeffrey Skinner's Theories and Inventions

To set your wake time on those old round-shouldered plastic clock radios, you had to twirl an extra hand around the clock face and line it up to the closest five minute interval. Tuning the radio was also a trick. You'd spin a dial that moved a pointer across frequencies spaced un-evenly over a translucent plexi window, music fuzzing on either side of the sweet spot. After these careful adjustments, you'd fall asleep to the tinny strains of the Temptations or Marvin Gaye, later waking to static, and wondering what movements in the moon or wind or clouds caused the radio waves to shift out of true. Back then we were used to things being close enough. There was room for error, and benefit of the doubt. Not like today's world where everything has been reduced to 1's and 0's or black and white. Where it's left or right, this or that, and nothing in-be-tween. Where I can't be right unless you are wrong. Where you set your clock to the minute, even as seconds keep ticking away.

Parallel Parking

Every night that week my dad drove us
to his office building's empty parking lot.
Still dressed in pinstripes,
he'd shove two garbage cans
onto icy pavement, then demonstrate
a perfect two-point maneuver.
My turn. I'd slide across the caddy's
cracked leather bench while he balanced
on crusty clumps of snow, a nimbus
of instructions billowing from his mouth.
Over and over I'd pull forward, then reverse
with clammy palms despite the brittle chill.
Most other nights he spent
behind his den's closed door,
but on these rare father-daughter dates
he beckoned me toward him
heedless of the slick street, the slippery curb.

Spackle

After church on Sundays
Dad made us stop at Sears.
He always needed something:
a rake, a screwdriver, bulbs
for outdoor lights. If he
could think of nothing else
he'd say he needed spackle.
Church-clothes itchy
we'd sweat in the Olds while Dad
jogged through double glass doors,
later emerging, spackle tub held aloft
as if it were a trophy.
Back home we'd scatter:
kickball for us kids,
Mom at her sewing machine,
Dad behind his den door,
head buried in briefcase,
spackle forgotten
on a high garage shelf.
Who can say what repair
he had in mind?
Our ceilings were smooth,
our walls unblemished
but he must have known
some holes needed filling.

Petrichor

After a storm, earthworms decorate streets
where they have slithered to avoid drowning
in rain-soaked soil. There they lie —
plumped tendrils, slender strands
stretched translucent over damp pavement.

Earless, eyeless, they hardly know
what peril their escape has brought.
They bask in the glow of survival
innocent of foot and tire,
naïve to sun on asphalt.

So many, there is barely space
for the wide toes of my running shoes.
I hop among them, heels up. Crouching,
I hook one on my finger and place it,
wriggling, onto protective grass.

My Friend, Pluto

We've been pals since high school,
Pluto and I, both of us spiraling
outside the periphery of the popular planets.
We were both puny in our own way,
with bumpy faces and uncontrollable gasses,
but we had our good points:
Pluto with his exceptional albedo,
and me, with my parlor trick talent for playing
the opening guitar riff to *Smoke on the Water*.
Eventually, we grew apart; I lost myself
in the chaos of young adulthood,
and Pluto withdrew into the aphelion
of his eccentric orbit.

Then, a few years ago,
I heard rumblings in the news.
Something about Pluto's mass being re-assessed.
It turns out the demotion wasn't about his mass
or even his slightly ovoid shape.
No, it came down to Pluto failing
to keep his neighborhood tidy,
leaving asteroids and comets in his wake
like a kid leaves dirty laundry
strewn across his bedroom floor.

I used to keep *my* neighborhood tidy.
I'd walk our street picking up cigarette butts,
crumpled burger wrappers

and the airline-sized vodka bottles
I suspect my unstable neighbor
secretly tossed back after midnight.
Yet always, the litter returned within a few days,
so finally I thought, *Screw it!*
Let the vodka bottles accumulate!

Maybe that's what happened with Pluto.
Heaven knows he has enough on his mind
what with maintaining a 2:3 resonance with Neptune
and keeping his argument of periapsis
librating at 90°. With that kind of schedule,
who has time to sweep up shattered remnants
of planetismals and clear out cosmic clouds?
Something's got to give and I, for one, am inclined
to cut Pluto a little slack.

After all, what's it matter if his orbit path is messy?
Everybody knows a little stardust never hurt anyone.

Shoo Fly

No matter how hard I try
I just cannot seem
to appreciate the fly.
It finds its way in
easily enough, depositing
who-knows-what
on all of my stuff.
You'd think it could leave
with similar ease,
but instead it just weaves
to and fro, bumping
incessantly against the window.
Try as I might to deliver
death's smite,
at the last possible moment
it always takes flight.
Yes, the fly keeps in motion
buzzed on some magic elixir,
'til finally it dies
inside my light fixture.
Though I do understand
that it's one of God's creatures,
the fly does not have
any redeeming features.

Opihi

A pleated parasol
fanned on the beach
its ridges cling to sand
resisting the pull
of receding waves.
It shields a pocket of space
sized for a minnow
a pearl
a seed washed ashore
from far away land.
I slip my fingernail
under its scalloped edge
and flip to reveal
no hidden prize,
just its underside
washed clean and smooth —
a shiny starburst
reflecting silvered gloam,
a tiny vessel
filled with the absence
of whatever called it home.

How It Comes to This

Peace Line Wall

Smog-colored concrete the height
of two men. Topped by ten
feet of corrugated green,
finished with a road's width
of wire screen, it's forty
feet tall, enough to block
a bomb or stop a brawl.
Street level murals scream
the failure of the political machine,
whose answer was the building of a wall
that brings no peace to Belfast at all.

Enlisted Men

I find a photo tucked inside the drawer
of Father's walnut desk. An army camp,
with soldiers dressed in olive green, their pant-
legs tucked in dusty boots. A threesome linked
by arms on shoulders, slouching side by side,
with goofy grins, a thumb upraised in mock
bravado. Standing well apart, my dad —
his oval face, his timid smile, the way
he slumps with hands on narrow hips, betray
him ill at ease. I wonder at this strange
tableau, his distance from their friendly knot,
as if he knew that he'd come home and they
would not.

Last Suppers

Inspired by Julie Green's art exhibit:
Final Meals of U.S. Death Row Inmates

Platters mounted on a museum wall
blue and white patterned like Dutch delft
imprinted with last meals of the condemned.

Prime rib and mashers, says one.
On another, lobster and cobbed corn.
Muted insight into stomachs and souls,
a reminder that killers like ice cream too.

It could be easy to dismiss these brutal men
unrepentant behind prison bars —
or so we picture them —
until a New York suffocation
or a snapped spine in Baltimore
tells us that too often,
guilt is gauged by skin tone.

I contemplate my own last meal wish:
peanut butter on toasted bread
salty chips and ice cold beer.
Simple fare to match simple wrongs
I think. But who's to say what favor
my fair complexion bought?

In Service

After a 2008 photo by Joao Silva

Black snow peppers cratered pavement.
Hours ago, a car bomb evaporated flesh
and bone into a brackish cloud.
Overcome by its own sooty weight,
it showered the street with human stain.

We step past police tape, fastidious
in our newly-issued army boots.
A pair of worn sandals lay
next to pieces of a wide leather strap
used to secure the bomb to the car
or to its driver.

It seems to me the crater
should be bigger.
It should be wide and deep enough
to bury the lost ambitions
of these people whose lives,
years ago, were unmolested.

I wonder how it comes to this —
me, standing on a Baghdad street
when only months ago,
I was secure at home, nightly
wrapped in my woman's arms,
daily tousling my boy's snow white hair.

Capital Airshow, September 11,

Ten Years After

I was in the north tower once
at Windows on the World.

Dizzied over rooftops
we pressed palms to glass

tracked the glint of an airplane
mirrored in the East River

asked what would happen to a penny
dropped from this height.

Now as I watch the TV replay
of billowing smoke

I hear the rumble of approaching aircraft
the buzzsaw whine as they cut overhead.

I wait, wrapped in stillness.
Is it happening again?

Shadows strobe my windows
splitting time into moments

the floor softens beneath my feet
and I am weightless, tumbling

remembering what they say —
that if you fall from a skyscraper

you'll never know what hit you
by the time you reach bottom.

The End Starts Before You Know It

One moment
you are following footprints
across a stale landscape
each step placed
in an exact perimeter
of hollowed sand.

Your toes slide sideways
the edge of your boot brushes a stone
only it isn't a stone and before you know it
a huge flash paints the air orange
glazes it with gray soot.

The last thing you see
your two best buddies —
stretcher bouncing between them —
hopping footprint to footprint
across red-splotched sand.

Now, a German hospital.
Here's your wife,
her smile forced.
The end of the bed
where your legs should be,
desert-flat.

She speaks of logistics —
rehab at Walter Reed

prosthetics
counseling for her, for you,
a car with hand controls.

Now you understand.
In that split second,
when you looked up
after some distant crack
echoed against the flat sky,
every decision was made.

Seeing Nancy Pelosi at Café de la Presse

February 2017

At first we didn't notice her, just the back
of her camel-hair coat ahead of us in line.
Then she turned to comment to her friend —

the full lips, the overly smooth skin —
Could it be her? we gasped as she was led
away from view. We savored our meal,

a medley of quinoa, chardonnay, dismay
about how rules and borders shift
as easily as sand.

A table away, the woman and her friend,
heads close over small plates,
murmured between themselves

strategizing, perhaps, or maybe just
debating over cherry tarte or mousse.
Eventually, she turned toward us to leave.

It's her, I said as two burly men,
discreet wires twisting to their ears,
appeared to guide her through the door

and to the curb where we saw
elegant legs tuck into a sleek
tinted car that swept away,

a Batmobile whisking Nancy off
to trade her beige coat
for black cape and pointy-eared mask,

appropriate attire
to save us from the Joker
as we can only hope.

Painting Trees

Painting Trees

My first has a stout trunk
with limbs dividing
upward and wide
as if waving songbirds in.
A cheerful tree, I decide.
Some gentle dabs
and leaves emerge,
emerald green layered over fern,
a few flecks of amber sunlight.

Next I try a somber tree:
slim stalk, grey scumbled bark,
and black streaks over brown
to indicate a shadowed side.
I brush in draped branches
berry-laden with orange daubs.
Or maybe those are blossoms.
Trees are forgiving that way;
a few smudges and whorls
and the imagination takes over.

Also, trees don't complain
about over-large crowns
or warty burls. Such things
don't matter to real trees,
which are indifferent to our gaze
and consumed with the hard work
of tree survival: layering bark
setting buds, drawing moisture
from our drying earth.

Reading Kwasny at 30,000 Feet

Inspired by Melissa Kwasny's Reading Novalis in Montana

First east, over ridges smoothed
by January snow, mountains of pleated silk.
At the foothills, a pointillist landscape of pines
scattered among brown and white spatters.
Then south — dormant, brindled fields split
into neat polygons drawn by tractor paths.
And pivots, perfectly turned
as if by a great hand.

They are grand in their wholeness
in a way that the crest, the tree, the furrow
when seen from ground level, are not.
Down there, it is the edgeless sky
that lifts the heart, expands the chest,
and though I am soaring through her big sky,
its thinness pervades,
its blue breadth diminished
by the portholes of this metal capsule.

Now we pass over the Great Salt Lake.
I see our silent shadow pierce
the clouds reflected in the rippled surface.
The sky is not one thing, I read,
but many highs and lows.

On the Train to La Spezia

An hour north of Pisa —

    past empty dresses shimmying from lines
        stretched between sooty stucco walls,

        meadow grasses swaying
           in the locomotive's wake,

    over unseen plates whose shift and scrape
        shaped fractured layers
           into exalted gathered robes,

    through Carrera
        where massive marble blocks
           lie trackside, sarcophagi

        enclosing dormant figures
           awaiting Buonarotti's chisel
                (but bound for kitchen counters
                in Spokane) —

A man jostles awake,
    gestures for my camera,
        snaps my face blurred before the glass

    while crisp, in the distance,
        the rived mountain's quarry
           glints like snow.

Backstage with Balkanski Circus Dancers

They lounge in camp chairs, iridescent brows
shimmering as if the spotlight followed
them here. Feathered in bright hues —
pink, purple, peach, aqua —
fringed bras, tufted tiara crests,
boas draped over crossed, graceful legs.

Like Degas' ballerinas portrayed
wearing frilled costumes splayed
over benches as they stretch,
adjust stockings and shoes,
while they go about the business
of not dancing, yet
observed by privileged patrons —

as I watch these dancers,
who don't so much ignore as dismiss me
while they chat among themselves,
one spreading wide her wings —
or rather, her arms —
describing some large thought
that has nothing to do
with dancing or birds.

W.S. Merwin and Monet

Sometimes I wonder if it's worth it —
all the weeding and mowing and pruning
it takes to keep our yard in trim.

Why not leave it wild, as it was
before we people came along
and decided we must tame it?

Picture Monet gesturing from a scaffold
to workers wielding picks against tangled brush
that would become his famous pond

with floating lilies, a wisteria-wrapped bridge.
As if he'd run out of beauty to paint
and had to make more of his own.

At the art museum, I wander among
his canvases, then pause by one
of splendid palms and think of Merwin

who just this day has died
after years of planting Maui soil
with sapling palms, remaking

wasted land — not to what
it was before — but to what
he thought it ought to be.

What swagger prompts the sculpted
boxwood hedge? The wire wrap
that stunts a bonsai's branch?

I look across our modest patch.
We like to think it's better now
with tidy shrubs and cultured blooms,

but how can we improve
on lacy shadows cast by sunlight
filtered through unruly trees?

Amethyst Brook

We came across a sylvan stream
And taking it as ours
Immersed ourselves, its cooling depths
Refreshing legs and arms.

We soon emerged, oblivious
Of waters we displaced,
Unmindful of our impudence,
In Nature's eye, disgraced.

By the River Before Dawn

Moonlight dusts a layer of fog,
the earth cushioned from above,
everything muffled or asleep.

It's a solace not to see beyond
the trail's next turn,
to linger under starless sky.

Sagebrush screens a path
winding to the river's bank.
Currents circle as if tarrying too.

55 years gone. 30, or so, to go —
the midpoint keeps moving.
Mostly, the way seems long.

Shoes slap against packed dirt
parting clusters of larkspur and thistle.
Kestrels dive the petals and spikes.

Ahead, the trail traces contours
of valley and slope. I push on
shouldering time's slow weight.

Letter to Kuusisto from California

Inspired by Stephen Kuusisto's Letters to Borges

It is autumn, and where you live
the patter of rain on leaves and earth
sounds like pennies dropped in mud.
Stephen, here in Sacramento
there has been no rain for months.
Although we can bike
or picnic any day we please,
our waterless creek beds
and brown pines stand silent.

path of totality

it sounds like the trail the Buddha trod
to reach the Bodhi tree

and that moment when the lotus
floats centered in the bowl

suspended as when the moon glides
before the sun and they appear as one

shimmer-ringed and true
though here in our valley

where alignment is askew
where fractional light casts

confused shadows to the ground
such a half-measure state

merely confounds
as to night fall or morning rise

and that brief hint
of an undivided day

disappears
as the moon slides away

Overcomplicating Things

Self-Portrait with Lemons

They're hidden by the back fence
behind hawthorn and pittosporum,
dwarfed by a twisted spruce.
Camouflaged so well, I'd nearly forgotten.
I pull on boots against the sodden grass,
then edge my shoulders between dripping branches.
There they are — studding the tree
like Christmas ornaments.
More, it seems, even than leaves.
It's clear they've waited overlong to be discovered;
settled juices have pulled them into teardrops,
their skins are nearly egg-yolk yellow.

Tomorrow we'll drag a ladder here and pick
bucket after bucket, ripe for giving to friends
as we admonish *use them soon*.
Later, I'll accept their emailed thanks,
addressed to Lemon Lady or in one case,
Lemon Tart, describing what they've made:
sugared squares, custard pie, zesty glaze.
Lemon Tart guy will infuse a batch of Limoncello
from which I'll hope to score a jar come summer.

It comforts me, this yearly twist and snap of stems,
the buckets left at doorsteps
for my small group of fellow lemonheads:
writers, drinkers, sometime-bakers —

all of us thriving, at least for a time,
from the same abundant tree.
When each crop's gone, the tree resets.
First, pink-tipped buds, then tiny pale blossoms
that don't smell lemony at all, whose heavy scent
anticipates next winter's weighted branches.

Daylight Savings

I hope that the hour
I get to live twice

is not spent sweeping
the entryway marble

scrubbing scum
off the bathtub rim

or polishing this sleek
walnut tabletop.

I rest my cheek against
its unblemished surface

and remember your palm
brushing my bare thigh

summer's supple heat
how our slide from grace

landed me here
where the hardness of things

echoes like thunder
where I am afraid

there are no second chances.

Marriage

A lacquered box.
Inside, a rattle of loose pearls,
their clasp, the frayed strand
that once tethered them.
In a wedding picture
they circle her slender throat
as she smiles up at the groom.
So lustrous against her pale skin,
it's easy to forget
there is sand at their centers,
that only the oyster's hard work
keeps the grains from chafing.

Moonlit

Tonight the moon hides tomorrow.
My son said *I am coming soon —*
when we are together I will know what you know.
See now, aspens dulled by pallid rays
all the leaves are voices
the moon hushes their whispering
sweeps silence through ghosted limbs
cloaks the mysteries awaiting your birth.
See how I am changed yet unchanged
branches tinged with silvered strands
until the milky light wanes
and the moon slides behind
the earth's swollen curve.

Homage to My Hair

after Lucille Clifton

This hair is big hair
it springs from my head
like sparks from a fire.
It's reckless
and a little bit dangerous
This hair makes you look.

This hair doesn't ask permission.
It thrusts its prickly filaments
into space, *your* space.
This hair, it penumbrates —
its tangled shadow
casts black lace
upon a white wall.

This hair is lawless —
impervious to mousse or spray,
it takes nothing lying down.
It won't be contained.
This hair shuns a hat.

When we sit close,
this hair scratches your chin.
And when I lean over you,
our bodies locked and moist,
this hair tickles the warm curve
of your naked belly.

Crossed Signals

1. Can you believe me when I tell you that *1* is white and so is *O*? *One* is also white. If you find this symmetry soothing, then I hope you are still with me when I say that *Won* is the color of mud, owing to its brown *W,* and that although *V* is half of *W,* it is not brown or even violet but dark cherry.

2. Some letters and numbers are colors for which there is no English word, not even *cerulean. D,* for instance, is the color of ocean under an overcast sky when there is light enough for depth but not reflection. Of *N,* Nabokov supposedly said "it is a greyish-yellowish oatmeal color." As if he didn't have enough trouble already, translating from the Russian.

3. Usually, a letter's color bleeds across the entire word. *F* is purple and so it follows that *frog* is purple, not mottled green as the amphibian would have it. Notwithstanding jonquils and doves, *flower* and *feather* are of amethyst hue. *Fear* and *freedom,* which might otherwise float invisibly through a colorless sky, are weighted by their purpleness.

4   I write these truths as if they are self-evident, but you regard me with suspicion. You point to black figures on a white page as if they are some sort of proof. They have nothing to do with this.

5. "Some colors reconcile themselves to one another, others just clash" (Edvard Munch). We can say the same of color and meaning. *Four* is purple. The four ball in billiards, purple. But *4* is copper. What are we to make of this? Tiny bombshells detonate in my brain with regularity.

6. Funny, you have always been the visual one; the one who sees how pieces fit together, who can assemble any new thing without reference to instructions. Yet you tell me you dream in concepts. That your dream-me is not my pale-faced blue-eyed self, rather the *idea* of me, an unseeable presence. What a disappointment, considering all the effort I have put into keeping trim.

7. I, on the other hand, dream in pictures; pictures whose colors are even more vivid than real life. Marauding yellows, reds and greens plunder my rest like loud and drunken party guests who have overstayed their welcome. "Everything is blooming most recklessly; if it were voices instead of colors, there would be an unbelievable shrieking into the heart of the night" (Rainer Maria Rilke). There are mornings when I awake relieved at the soft-filtered light casting greyness on my bedroom. On these days, I dress in monochrome beige or blue. "One of my favorite colors is no color at all" (Billy Baldwin).

8. You accuse me of overcomplicating things. It's simple, you explain, how a prism splits light into neat rainbow swaths. How colors disappear in darkness. I try to see it your way, but your kaleidoscope words dazzle my view.

Outside the Box

On a day
when river-glass
reflects the willows' sway,
and timid breeze perfects
the air with sweet
gardenia scent,
and rapt lizards bask
on heat infused stone,

it's a sin
to be trapped
within a fluorescent
cell, hemmed in
by a laminate flat
hooked to half walls
mute with padded cloth.
On such a fine day
there is no better argument
for sloth.

Toolbox Letters

They are softened by years
spent in his machinists' toolbox
alongside calipers, end mills, an edge finder —
tools he now removes one by one,
wipes down, then carefully replaces.
He won't need them anytime soon.

He hands me the fistful of wilted papers
haphazardly folded, a tradesman's origami.
It takes just a beat for me to realize
these are the letters he wrote during breaks.
In case I ever get hurt, he once explained,
I want you to know how I feel.

I think I already know
for he's shown me in countless ways —
this man who trades in fixes and feelings
over valentines or roses.
My husband, dismissed today
after decades of harsh labor,

whose skilled hands mastered
every tool except a pen,
offers me this stack of messy notes.
It's hard to fathom what words
could better smooth my crumpled heart
but I accept the smudged pages
then tuck them away, unread.

Everything Keeps Shifting

Distant

My mother told me how the cat chased
his catnip mouse under the dresser,
and about the coming snow,
and I, after making sure she had groceries
and generator fuel, hung up the phone reassured.

Later she said the falling snow had reached
10 inches, and though it was a fairyland outside,
the cat was cross about it, especially after having
earlier lost his catnip mouse under the dresser.

Today, the UPS man delivered the box she sent.
One by one, I unwrap the gifts
she made in pottery class. A pair of mugs,
the handles like two halves of a valentine.
A platter with her thumbprints scalloping its edges.

Most beautiful of all, a shallow bowl
shaped like a leaf, each lobe gently upturned
and etched like a palm's lifeline. So delicate,
I am amazed it arrived unbroken.

I call to tell her the box showed up safely
and again she explains: cat, mouse, dresser.

Transition, Spring

It's only March, but already it's a madhouse
at the garden center. I wend my cart
through a throng of green thumbs
and picture you in Pennsylvania
with snow up to your hubcaps,
ice fangs jawing your door.
Everything frozen in place
as if winter wants to keep you
forever.

Kneeling in what will soon be your garden
I sink my trowel under the tall pine,
press each plant into loosened earth.
Your favorite pink begonias,
coleus with extravagant red-trimmed
leaves, fuchsia's nodding bells,
all rooting in California soil.

Apples and Tomatoes

As I pick the last of summer's heirlooms,
I also gather apples scattered by the tree.
They have fallen too early,
their yellow-green skins barely blushed
around the stems, bruises hastening decay.

This tree produced just one generous bounty —
buckets of sweet our first year here.
After its second stingy crop
we tried humus, mulch, careful pruning,
watering more, then less.
Still the tree drops its fruit as if to say
there's nothing you can do.

My mother watches from our shaded porch.
She accepts a share of Brandywines
but scowls at the puny Gravensteins I offer.
You wouldn't eat them growing up, she says.
I wonder which she means, but now
she's telling me about the snow-draped pine
outside her old front door, how California days
are much too long and all the same.

Next week, or maybe in a month,
we'll pull the vines and tamp the soil.
For now she rests, and together
we sort apples in the day's subtracting light.

He Grows Old

He points
at himself
then points
at the headline
then again
at himself.
Then breaks
into laughter
by which
we realize
he has told
us a joke.
Not his old
favorite
about three men in
a bar
but a gag
that plays
on his own
riddled state.
Funny —
we're slow
catching
his keen
wordless jest
its punchline
surprising
as any
good joke.

He wakes
tangled
in twisted
sheets
shouting
for someone
to save him
from hulking
shadows
surrounding
his narrow bed,
from black
demons looming
in his dreams,
the two
indistinguishable
and equally
frightening
under night's
heavy cloak.

He takes
small steps
each foot
barely
clearing
the floor
as he shuffles
forward
like a blind man
avoiding
walls
or a traveler
on an icy path.
Even though
his thick
soled shoes
land
on solid
ground
he falters
as everything
around him
keeps shifting.

Early Blizzard

The x-ray image is almost beautiful.
Within the bell-shaped outline of lungs
a thick stalk, white with what could be snow,
and outstretched branches likewise flocked.
The doctor says the dark spaces in-between
will whiten eventually, too.
As with any inclement weather,
the timing is unpredictable —
like the day an early blizzard
forced our family to leave the car
and climb the long hill leading to our house.
Dad lifted me onto his shoulders
out of the snow's ponderous drifts
into a weightless snow-globe sky.
Back then I thought he was the tallest
man around, the strongest too,
and steadfast as our maple's icy trunk.
He could save us from anything
and did, and still would,
even though his shoulders curve
around his stiffened chest,
and he stands braced
against a gathering storm.

Forward Light

. . . darkness doesn't war against the light
it comes forward
to another light

Yehuda Amichai

The phone call comes after darkness
settles, when I am alone. It doesn't
seem real, this news of my father at war
with his own body. I lean my head against
the window and it seems as if the blackness on the
other side might break the glass and thicken this light.
Many days will pass before we know how it
ends—whether the tubes that feed Dad's veins, the one that comes
from his mouth, are enough to rally his troops forward.
We circle his bed wondering what to
make of his flickering eyelids. Perhaps he sees another
kind of window, another kind of light.

It's not as if you have to drink the sea

Ce n'est pas la mer à boire
is what they say in France to mean

it's not so bad or, as we might say,
it's not the end of the world.

For a time, land, sea and sky blur
in grayscale. No discernible horizon.

Then I find a hillside's soft ochre folds
and this sheared limestone cliff

that might have been earth's edge
except I'm here, standing in its shadow.

Lavender echoes through the canyon
and across this pasture where two donkeys amble

to the fence and show their donkey teeth.
I feed them fistfuls of long grass.

Their simple joy makes me grateful too:
for strong legs that carry me past

neat rows of yellowing vines,
for dry-stacked stone walls

ordering olive groves
and fields lavish with fruit.

Thankful for the boldness
of great Pyrenees protecting their sheep

and for tiny white snails
drawing moisture from damp swaying stalks.

Words Escape Her

for Theresa McCourt

This morning she sits at her notebook, absorbed in the effort of arranging and re-arranging words, forming pleasing combinations of rhythm and meaning, sentences entwined like garlands. When she puts down her pen, she'll unfurl her mat and assume yoga poses — Dandasana, Utkatasana, and a host of other 'asanas' she will soon no longer remember. Yet she can see them in her mind's eye and translate them to her body, cherishing the reaching and the bending in the here and now. The twisting and balancing in three dimensions. Later, she will go outside where her autumn garden speaks through browned blossoms and tangled stems. Where the faint scent of decay and the dampened knees of her jeans tell her everything she needs to know about the condition of the soil. She'll wield clippers and trowel, perform the fall rituals that assure next summer's harvest. One day soon, she'll return to her notebook and try to understand what is written there, the once vibrant meaning lost among withered neurons. The script, merely marks and spaces. Perhaps she'll take pleasure in their pattern on the page, like the orderly rows of trees in the orchard, or migrating geese in their southbound V — beautiful, unencumbered by the weight of words.

A Second Life

From his wheelchair, Matisse cut painted paper into shapes he arranged and re-arranged against plain backgrounds. Greens like young grasses, yellows as yellow as a new day. Firethorn orange, red and solid black. Flower of flowers, leaf of leaves, loose-fingered pieces fit together untethered by stem or petiole. Release the mind and the body follows. Like the blue nudes: supple muscles absent bones, limbs wrapping limbs. Limbs flung to reveal a body's jazz — a body suspended like a swing note that separates before and after. Like the beat off-beat of a restarted heart.

Notes

Some poems are inspired by, or loosely modeled after other people's poems.

Spring Fancy	Mary Oliver
Theory of Absolutes	Jeffrey Skinner
Reading Kwasny	Melissa Kwasny
Amethyst Brook	Emily Dickinson
Letter to Kuusisto	Stephen Kuusisto
Homage to My Hair	Lucille Clifton
Crossed Signals	Maggie Nelson

Many thanks to the following publications in which some of these poems have appeared:

American River Review

Blast Furnace

The Cape Rock

Convergence

Fourth and Sycamore

Garrison Keillor's First Person

Late Peaches

Poeming Pigeon

Poetry Now

Rattlesnake Review

Sacramento Voices

Silver Birch Press

Soul of the Narrator

Susurrus